The Envelope Please

We're delighted to present the ten best ways to add a burst of color and texture to your home! Carolyn Pfeifer's pillows to knit are all created with envelope-style flaps and finished with decorative buttons. Each design has instructions to fit 14" square, 16" square, or 12" x 16" rectangular purchased pillow forms. The cozy, modern cushions are also the odds-on favorites for thoughtful housewarming gifts!

TABLE OF CONTENTS

Meet the Designer

Carolyn Pfeifer has a passion for knitting. "I have a beauty salon," she says, "and the unused spaces of my shop are great for yarn storage! When I have a break between clients, I work on my projects."

Carolyn learned to knit in high school, but as a designer, she had to set it aside for a few decades.
She says, "For a while, patterns for knitting were not in high demand. I enjoyed developing crochet designs for Leisure Arts and for several yarn craft magazines. But I wanted to get back to knitting, so I finally started designing for the needles. One day, I saw an envelope pillow made of fabric. I started drawing up flap designs.

"The body of each knitted envelope pillow is one piece, just sewn up the sides. All the flaps are Stockinette Stitch, and the knitter can change out the flaps if she wants more style options. Design ideas are abundant for me," Carolyn says. "I enjoy all yarn crafts, but I'm excited to be knitting again."

LEISURE ARTS, INC.
Maumelle, Arkansas

Two Color Slip Stitch

EASY

Finished Sizes:

12" x 16" (30.5 cm x 40.5 cm)
14" x 14" (35.5 cm x 35.5 cm)
16" x 16" (40.5 cm x 40.5 cm)

Size Note: Instructions are written for 12" x 16" size, with sizes 14" x 14", and 16" x 16" in braces { }. Instructions will be easier to read if you circle all the numbers pertaining to your size. If only one number is given, it applies to all sizes.

SHOPPING LIST

Yarn (Medium Weight) MEDIUM 4

[3.5 ounces, 210 yards
(100 grams, 192 meters) per skein**]**:

- ☐ Grey - 2{2-3} skeins
- ☐ Green - 1{1-2} skein(s)

Knitting Needles

- ☐ Straight, size 8 (5 mm)

or size needed for gauge

Additional Supplies

- ☐ Pillow form - 12" x 16" {14" square - 16" square} / 30.5 cm x 40.5 cm {35.5 cm square - 40.5 cm square}
- ☐ Yarn needle
- ☐ 1½" (38 mm) Buttons - 2
- ☐ $^{7}/_{8}$" (22 mm) Buttons - 2

Techniques used:

- Slip 1, K1, PSSO *(Fig. 1, page 44)*
- K2 tog *(Fig. 2, page 44)*

GAUGE: In pattern,
23 sts and 33 rows = 4" (10 cm)

Gauge Swatch: 4" square (10 cm)
Cast on 23 sts.
Work same as Body for 33 rows.
Bind off all sts in **purl**.

Pillow is made in one piece with the body worked in pattern stitch and the flap worked in Stockinette Stitch. Begin pillow at top edge, behind Flap.

BODY

With Green, cast on 93{81-93} sts.

Row 1 (Right side)**:** Slip 1 as if to **knit**, ★ WYF slip 1 as if to **purl**, WYB K1; repeat from ★ across.

Loop a short piece of yarn around any stitch to mark Row 1 as **right** side.

Row 2: Slip 1 as if to **knit**, purl across; drop Green, do **not** cut yarn.

Row 3: With Grey, slip 1 as if to **purl**, ★ WYB K1, WYF slip 1 as if to **purl**; repeat from ★ across to last 2 sts, K2.

Row 4: Slip 1 as if to **knit**, purl across; drop Grey, do **not** cut yarn.

Row 5: With Green, slip 1 as if to **knit**, ★ WYF slip 1 as if to **purl**, WYB K1; repeat from ★ across.

Repeat Rows 2-5 until piece measures 24{28-32}" / 61{71-81} cm, ending by working Row 2.

Cut Green.

FLAP

Rows 1-3: Knit across.

Row 4: Purl across.

Row 5 (Decrease row)**:** K1, slip 1 as if to **knit**, K1, PSSO, knit across to last 3 sts, K2 tog, K1: 91{79-91} sts.

Working in Stockinette Stitch (knit one row, purl one row), continue to decrease one stitch at each edge, every fourth row, 8 times **more,** then decrease every other row, 9{10-9} times: 57{43-57} sts.

Bind off all sts in **purl**.

FINISHING

Steam Flap to block.

With **wrong** sides together, fold Body so that cast on edge meets base of Flap. With yarn needle and Grey, whipstitch sides of Body together ***(Fig. 7, page 46)***.
Insert pillow form, then stitch the cast on edge to the base of the Flap.

To anchor Flap, sew smaller buttons to Flap **and** Body approximately 1" (2.5 cm) from the side edges of Flap; sew larger buttons through both thicknesses, evenly spaced between the smaller buttons.

Twisted Garter Stitch

INTERMEDIATE

Finished Sizes:
12" x 16" (30.5 cm x 40.5 cm)
14" x 14" (35.5 cm x 35.5 cm)
16" x 16" (40.5 cm x 40.5 cm)

Size Note: Instructions are written for 12" x 16" size, with sizes 14" x 14", and 16" x 16" in braces { }. Instructions will be easier to read if you circle all the numbers pertaining to your size. If only one number is given, it applies to all sizes.

SHOPPING LIST

Yarn (Medium Weight)

MEDIUM 4

[3.5 ounces, 210 yards
(100 grams, 192 meters) per skein**]**:

- ☐ Tan - 2{2-3} skeins
- ☐ Brown Marl - 1{1-2} skein(s)

Knitting Needles

- ☐ Straight, sizes 8 (5 mm) **and** 9 (5.5 mm) **or** sizes needed for gauge

Additional Supplies

- ☐ Pillow form - 12" x 16" {14" square - 16" square} / 30.5 cm x 40.5 cm {35.5 cm square - 40.5 cm square}
- ☐ Yarn needle
- ☐ 7/8" (22 mm) Buttons - 5

26 THURS
WRITING CAMP

Techniques used:

- Slip 1, K1, PSSO *(Fig. 1, page 44)*
- K2 tog *(Fig. 2, page 44)*
- K2 tog tbl *(Fig. 3, page 44)*

GAUGE: With larger size needles, in pattern, 24 sts and 26 rows = 4" (10 cm)

Gauge Swatch: 4" square (10 cm)
With larger size needles, cast on 24 sts.
Work same as Body for 26 rows.
Bind off all sts in **knit**.

Pillow is made in one piece with the Body worked in pattern stitch and the Flap in Stockinette Stitch. Begin pillow at top edge, behind Flap.

BODY

With Tan and larger size needles, cast on 99{87-99} sts.

Row 1: ★ K1, K2 tog tbl, do **not** slip sts from needle, knit the **same** 2 sts tog through front loops and slip from needle; repeat from ★ across.

Repeat Row 1 for pattern until piece measures 24{28-32}" / 61{71-81} cm.

Cut Tan.

FLAP

Change to smaller size needles.

Rows 1-3: With Brown Marl, knit across.

Row 4: K1, purl across.

Row 5 (Decrease row - Right side)**:** K1, slip 1 as if to **knit**, K1, PSSO, knit across: 98{86-98} sts.

Loop a short piece of yarn around any stitch to mark Row 5 as **right** side.

Row 6: K1, purl across.

Rows 7-16: Repeat Rows 5 and 6, 5 times: 93{81-93} sts.

Row 17 (Decrease row)**:** K1, (slip 1 as if to **knit**, K1, PSSO) twice, knit across: 91{79-91} sts.

Row 18: K1, purl across.

Rows 19 thru 34{36-38}: Repeat Rows 17 and 18, 8{9-10} times: 75{61-71} sts.

Bind off all sts in **knit**.

FINISHING

Steam Flap to block.

With **wrong** sides together, fold Body so that cast on edge meets base of Flap. With yarn needle and Tan, whipstitch sides of Body together ***(Fig. 7, page 46)***. Insert pillow form, then stitch the cast on edge to the base of the Flap.

To anchor Flap, sew buttons to Flap **and** Body, spacing evenly along bound off edge.

Basketweave

EASY

Finished Sizes:

12" x 16" (30.5 cm x 40.5 cm)

14" x 14" (35.5 cm x 35.5 cm)

16" x 16" (40.5 cm x 40.5 cm)

Size Note: Instructions are written for 12" x 16" size, with sizes 14" x 14", and 16" x 16" in braces { }. Instructions will be easier to read if you circle all the numbers pertaining to your size. If only one number is given, it applies to all sizes.

SHOPPING LIST

Yarn (Medium Weight) MEDIUM 4

[3 ounces, 158 yards (85 grams, 144 meters) per skein]:

- ☐ Lt Grey - 2{2-3} skeins
- ☐ Dk Grey - 1 skein

Knitting Needles

- ☐ Straight, sizes 7 (4.5 mm) **and** 8 (5 mm) **or** sizes needed for gauge

Additional Supplies

- ☐ Crochet hook, size H (5 mm) (for fringe)
- ☐ Pillow form - 12" x 16" {14" square - 16" square} / 30.5 cm x 40.5 cm {35.5 cm square - 40.5 cm square}
- ☐ Cardboard (for fringe)
- ☐ Yarn needle
- ☐ 5/8" (22 mm) Buttons - 3

Techniques used:

- Slip 1, K1, PSSO *(Fig. 1, page 44)*
- K2 tog *(Fig. 2, page 44)*

GAUGE: With larger size needles, in pattern, 20 sts and 29 rows = 4" (10 cm)

Gauge Swatch: 4½" w x 4" h (11.5 cm x 10 cm)
With larger size needles, cast on 23 sts.
Work same as Body for 29 rows.
Bind off all sts in **knit**.

Pillow is made in one piece with the Body worked in pattern stitch and the Flap in Stockinette Stitch. Begin pillow at top edge, behind Flap.

BODY

With Lt Grey and larger size needles, cast on 83{73-83} sts.

Row 1 (Right side)**:** K3, (P7, K3) across.

Loop a short piece of yarn around any stitch to mark Row 1 as **right** side.

Row 2: P3, (K7, P3) across.

Row 3: K3, (P7, K3) across.

Row 4: Purl across.

Row 5: P5, K3, (P7, K3) across to last 5 sts, P5.

Row 6: K5, P3, (K7, P3) across to last 5 sts, K5.

Row 7: P5, K3, (P7, K3) across to last 5 sts, P5.

Row 8: Purl across.

Repeat Rows 1-8 for pattern until piece measures 24{28-32}" / 61{71-81} cm, ending by working Row 4 or Row 8.

Cut Lt Grey.

FLAP

Change to smaller size needles.

Rows 1-3: With Dk Grey, knit across.

Row 4: K1, purl across to last st, K1.

Row 5: Knit across.

Rows 6 thru 30{36-42}: Repeat Rows 4 and 5, 12{15-18} times; then repeat Row 4 once **more**.

Bind off all sts in **knit**.

FINISHING

Steam Flap to block.

With **wrong** sides together, fold Body so that cast on edge meets base of Flap. With yarn needle and Lt Grey, whipstitch sides of Body together *(Fig. 7, page 46)*. Insert pillow form, then stitch the cast on edge to the base of the Flap.

FRINGE

Cut a piece of cardboard 5" (12.5 cm) wide and 2" (5 cm) long. Wind Dk Grey loosely and evenly lengthwise around the cardboard until the card is filled, then cut across one end; repeat as needed. Fold one strand in half. With **wrong** side facing and using a crochet hook, draw the folded end up through a stitch and pull the loose ends through the folded end *(Fig. A)*; draw the knot up tightly *(Fig. B)*. Repeat in each st across bound off edge. Lay flat on a hard surface and trim the ends.

Fig. A

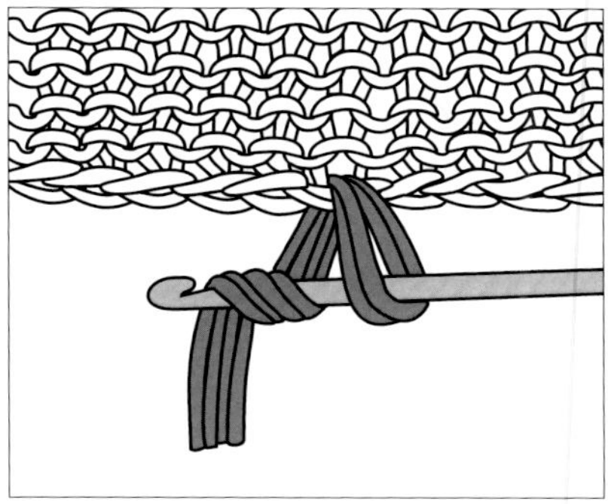

Fig. B

To anchor Flap, sew one button to center of Flap **and** Body ¼" (7 mm) above fringe; sew remaining two buttons approximately 2" (5 cm) to right and left of center button.

Broken Rib Stitch

EASY

Finished Sizes:
12" x 16" (30.5 cm x 40.5 cm)
14" x 14" (35.5 cm x 35.5 cm)
16" x 16" (40.5 cm x 40.5 cm)

Size Note: Instructions are written for 12" x 16" size, with sizes 14" x 14", and 16" x 16" in braces { }. Instructions will be easier to read if you circle all the numbers pertaining to your size. If only one number is given, it applies to all sizes.

SHOPPING LIST

Yarn (Medium Weight) MEDIUM 4

[3.5 ounces, 210 yards
(100 grams, 192 meters) per skein**]**:
- ☐ Purple - 3 skeins
- ☐ Dk Purple - 1 skein

Knitting Needles

- ☐ Straight, size 9 (5.5 mm)
  or size needed for gauge

Additional Supplies

- ☐ Pillow form - 12" x 16" {14" square - 16" square} / 30.5 cm x 40.5 cm {35.5 cm square - 40.5 cm square}
- ☐ Yarn needle
- ☐ 1½" (38 mm) Button - 1

Techniques used:

- Slip 1, K1, PSSO *(Fig. 1, page 44)*
- K2 tog *(Fig. 2, page 44)*

GAUGE: In pattern,
18 sts and 26 rows = 4" (10 cm)

Gauge Swatch:
4¼" w x 4" h (11 x 10 cm)
Cast on 19 sts.
Work same as Body for 26 rows.
Bind off all sts in **knit**.

Pillow is made in one piece with the Body worked in pattern stitch and the Flap in Stockinette Stitch. Begin pillow at top edge, behind Flap.

BODY

With Purple, cast on 74{64-74} sts.

Row 1 (Right side)**:** K3, P3, (K2, P3) across to last 3 sts, K3.

Loop a short piece of yarn around any stitch to mark Row 1 as **right** side.

Row 2: K1, purl across to last st, K1.

Repeat Rows 1 and 2 for pattern until piece measures 24{28-32}" / 61{71-81} cm, ending by working Row 2.

Cut Purple.

FLAP

Cut a 50" (127 cm) length of Dk Purple and set aside.

Rows 1-3: With Dk Purple, knit across.

Row 4: K1, purl across to last st, K1.

Row 5: Knit across.

Rows 6 thru 26{30-40}: Repeat Rows 4 and 5, 10{12-17} times; then repeat Row 4 once **more**.

POINT

Row 1: Bind off first 26{21-26} sts in **purl** (one stitch remains on right needle), K 21, drop yarn; with cut length, bind off last 26{21-26} sts in **purl**: 22 sts.

Row 2: K1, purl across to last st, K1.

Row 3: K1, slip 1 as if to **knit**, K1, PSSO, knit across to last 3 sts, K2 tog, K1: 20 sts.

Rows 4-12: Repeat Rows 2 and 3, 4 times; then repeat Row 2 once **more**: 12 sts.

Row 13: K1, (slip 1 as if to **knit**, K1, PSSO) twice, K2, K2 tog twice, K1: 8 sts.

Rows 14-17: Repeat Rows 2 and 3 twice: 4 sts.

Bind off all sts in **knit**.

FINISHING

Steam Flap to block.

With **wrong** sides together, fold Body so that cast on edge meets base of Flap. With yarn needle and Purple, whipstitch sides of Body together ***(Fig. 7, page 46)***. Insert pillow form, then stitch the cast on edge to the base of the Flap.

To anchor Flap, sew button to Flap **and** Body 1" (2.5 cm) above base of Point.

Star Stitch

INTERMEDIATE

Finished Sizes:

12" x 16" (30.5 cm x 40.5 cm)
14" x 14" (35.5 cm x 35.5 cm)
16" x 16" (40.5 cm x 40.5 cm)

Size Note: Instructions are written for 12" x 16" size, with sizes 14" x 14", and 16" x 16" in braces { }. Instructions will be easier to read if you circle all the numbers pertaining to your size. If only one number is given, it applies to all sizes.

SHOPPING LIST

Yarn (Medium Weight) MEDIUM 4

[3 ounces, 132 yards
(85 grams, 120 meters) per skein**]**:

- ☐ White - 2 skeins
- ☐ Black - 2 skeins

Knitting Needles

- ☐ Straight, size 9 (5.5 mm)
  or size needed for gauge

Additional Supplies

- ☐ Pillow form - 12" x 16" {14" square - 16" square} / 30.5 cm x 40.5 cm {35.5 cm square - 40.5 cm square}
- ☐ Yarn needle
- ☐ 1" (25 mm) Button - 1

Techniques used:

- Slip 1, K1, PSSO *(Fig. 1, page 44)*
- K2 tog *(Fig. 2, page 44)*
- P3 tog *(Fig. 5, page 45)*
- YO *(Fig. 6a, page 45)*

GAUGE: In pattern,
25 sts and 22 rows = 4" (10 cm)

Gauge Swatch: 4" square (10 cm)
Cast on 25 sts.
Work same as Body for 22 rows.
Bind off all sts in **knit**.

Pillow is made in one piece with the Body worked in pattern stitch and the Flap in Stockinette Stitch. Begin pillow at top edge, behind Flap.

BODY

With White, cast on 101{89-101} sts.

Row 1 (Right side)**:** Knit across.

Loop a short piece of yarn around any stitch to mark Row 1 as **right** side.

Row 2: P1, ★ P3 tog, do **not** slip sts from needle, YO, purl the **same** 3 sts tog and slip from needle, P1; repeat from ★ across; drop White, do **not** cut yarn.

Row 3: With Black, knit across.

Row 4: P3, P3 tog, do **not** slip sts from needle, YO, purl the **same** 3 sts tog and slip from needle, ★ P1, P3 tog, do **not** slip sts from needle, YO, purl the **same** 3 sts tog and slip from needle; repeat from ★ across to last 3 sts, P3; drop Black, do **not** cut yarn.

Row 5: With White, knit across.

Repeat Rows 2-5 for pattern until piece measures 24{28-32}" / 61{71-81} cm, ending by working Row 4.

Cut Black.

FLAP

Rows 1-3: With White, knit across.

Row 4: Purl across.

Row 5: (Slip 1 as if to **knit**, K1, PSSO) twice, knit across to last 4 sts, K2 tog twice: 97{85-97} sts.

Rows 6 thru 52{46-52}: Repeat Rows 4 and 5, 23{20-23} times; then repeat Row 4 once **more**: 5 sts.

Last Row: Slip 1 as if to **knit**, K1, PSSO, K1, K2 tog: 3 sts.

Bind off all sts in **knit**.

FINISHING

Steam Flap to block.

With **wrong** sides together, fold Body so that cast on edge meets base of Flap. With yarn needle and White, whipstitch sides of Body together ***(Fig. 7, page 46)***. Insert pillow form, then stitch the cast on edge to the base of the Flap.

To anchor Flap, sew one button to center of Flap **and** Body ¾" (19 mm) above point; sew remaining button to Body approximately 1¼" (3.25 cm) below point.

Cut 4, 12" (30.5 cm) lengths of Black. Holding strands together, fasten one end to a stationary object or have another person hold it; twist until tight. Fold in half and let it twist itself. Knot ends together forming loop. Wrap loop around upper button, then twist loop and wrap around lower button. Secure ends inside pillow.

Lace Ribbing

INTERMEDIATE

Finished Sizes:

12" x 16" (30.5 cm x 40.5 cm)
14" x 14" (35.5 cm x 35.5 cm)
16" x 16" (40.5 cm x 40.5 cm)

Size Note: Instructions are written for 12" x 16" size, with sizes 14" x 14", and 16" x 16" in braces { }. Instructions will be easier to read if you circle all the numbers pertaining to your size. If only one number is given, it applies to all sizes.

SHOPPING LIST

Yarn (Medium Weight) MEDIUM 4

[3.5 ounces, 210 yards
(100 grams, 192 meters) per skein**]:**

- ☐ 2{2-3} skeins

Knitting Needles

- ☐ Straight, size 8 (5 mm)
  or size needed for gauge

Additional Supplies

- ☐ Pillow form - 12" x 16" {14" square - 16" square} / 30.5 cm x 40.5 cm {35.5 cm square - 40.5 cm square}
- ☐ Yarn needle
- ☐ $1^1/_8$" (30 mm) Buttons - 2

Techniques used:

- Slip 1, K1, PSSO *(Fig. 1, page 44)*
- K2 tog *(Fig. 2, page 44)*
- P2 tog *(Fig. 4, page 44)*
- YO *(Fig. 6b, page 45)*

GAUGE: In pattern,
22 sts and 28 rows = 4" (10 cm)

Gauge Swatch: 4" square (10 cm)
Cast on 22 sts.
Row 1: K6, P1, (K1, P2) 3 times, K6.
Row 2: P6, K1, (P2, K1) 3 times, P6.
Row 3: K6, P1, (K1, YO, P2 tog) 3 times, K6.
Row 4: P6, K1, (P2, K1) 3 times, P6.
Row 5: K6, P1, (K1, P2) 3 times, K6.
Row 6: P6, K1, (YO, P2 tog, K1) 3 times, P6.
Rows 7-28: Repeat Rows 1-6, 3 times; then repeat Rows 1-4 once more.

Pillow is made in one piece with the Body worked in pattern stitch and the Flap in Stockinette Stitch. Begin pillow at top edge, behind Flap.

BODY

Cast on 91{75-91} sts.

Rows 1 and 2: Purl across.

Row 3 (Right side)**:** K2, P2, (K1, P2) twice, ★ K6, P1, (K1, P2) 3 times; repeat from ★ across to last st, K1.

Loop a short piece of yarn around any stitch to mark Row 3 as **right** side.

Row 4: K2, P2, (K1, P2) twice, ★ K1, P6, (K1, P2) 3 times; repeat from ★ across to last st, K1.

Row 5: K2, YO, P2 tog, (K1, YO, P2 tog) twice, ★ K6, P1, (K1, YO, P2 tog) 3 times; repeat from ★ across to last st, K1.

Row 6: K2, P2, (K1, P2) twice, ★ K1, P6, (K1, P2) 3 times; repeat from ★ across to last st, K1.

Row 7: K2, P2, (K1, P2) twice, ★ K6, P1, (K1, P2) 3 times; repeat from ★ across to last st, K1.

Row 8: K2, (YO, P2 tog, K1) 3 times, ★ P6, (K1, YO, P2 tog) 3 times, K1; repeat from ★ across.

Repeat Rows 3-8 for pattern until piece measures 24{28-32}" / 61{71-81} cm, ending by working a **wrong** side row.

Do **not** cut yarn.

FLAP

Rows 1-3: Knit across.

Row 4: K1, purl across to last st, K1.

Row 5: Knit across.

Rows 6-28: Repeat Rows 4 and 5, 11 times; then repeat Row 4 once **more**.

Row 29: K2{1-2}, (slip 1 as if to **knit**, K1, PSSO, K1) 14{12-14} times, K3{1-3}, (K2tog, K1) 14{12-14} times, K2{1-2}: 63{51-63} sts.

Row 30: K1, purl to last st, K1.

Row 31: K1, (slip 1 as if to **knit**, K1, PSSO, K1)10{8-10} times, K1, (K2tog, K1) 10{8-10} times, K1: 43{35-43) sts.

Row 32: K1, purl across to last st, K1.

Row 33: Knit across.

Rows 34 thru 48{52-54}: Repeat Rows 32 and 33, 7{9-10} times; then repeat Row 32 once **more**.

Bind off all sts in **purl**.

FINISHING

Steam Flap to block.

With **wrong** sides together, fold Body so that cast on edge meets base of Flap. With yarn needle, whipstitch sides of Body together ***(Fig. 7, page 46)***. Insert pillow form, then stitch the cast on edge to the base of the Flap.

To anchor Flap, sew buttons to Flap **and** Body ¾" (19 mm) above bound off edge and 1" (2.5 cm) in from side edges of Flap.

Zig Zag Angles

INTERMEDIATE

Finished Sizes:

12" x 16" (30.5 cm x 40.5 cm)
14" x 14" (35.5 cm x 35.5 cm)
16" x 16" (40.5 cm x 40.5 cm)

Size Note: Instructions are written for 12" x 16" size, with sizes 14" x 14", and 16" x 16" in braces { }. Instructions will be easier to read if you circle all the numbers pertaining to your size. If only one number is given, it applies to all sizes.

SHOPPING LIST

Yarn (Medium Weight) MEDIUM 4

[3 ounces, 158 yards
(85 grams, 144 meters) per skein**]**:

- ☐ Green - 2{2-3} skeins
- ☐ Brown - 1 skein

Knitting Needles

- ☐ Straight, size 8 (5 mm)
  or size needed for gauge

Additional Supplies

- ☐ Pillow form - 12" x 16" {14" square - 16" square} / 30.5 cm x 40.5 cm {35.5 cm square - 40.5 cm square}
- ☐ Yarn needle
- ☐ 7/8" (22 mm) Button - 1

Techniques used:

- Slip 1, K1, PSSO *(Fig. 1, page 44)*
- K2 tog *(Fig. 2, page 44)*

GAUGE: In pattern,
21 sts and 28 rows = 4" (10 cm)

Gauge Swatch: 4" square (10 cm)
Cast on 21 sts.
Row 1: K6, P5, K5, P5.
Row 2: K4, P5, K5, P5, K2.
Row 3: K1, P2, K5, P5, K5, P3.
Row 4: K2, P5, K5, P5, K4.
Row 5: K1, P4, K5, P5, K5, P1.
Row 6: P5, K5, P5, K6.
Row 7: K1, (P5, K5) twice.
Rows 8 and 9: (K5, P5) twice, K1.
Row 10: P2, K5, P5, K5, P3, K1.
Row 11: K3, P5, K5, P5, K3.
Row 12: P4, K5, P5, K5, P1, K1.
Row 13: K1, (P5, K5) twice.
Row 14: P5, K5, P5, K6.
Rows 15-28: Repeat Rows 1-14.
Bind off all sts in **knit**.

Pillow is made in one piece with the Body worked in pattern stitch and the Flap in Stockinette Stitch. Begin pillow at top edge, behind Flap.

BODY

With Green, cast on 87{77-87} sts.

Rows 1 and 2: Purl across.

Row 3 (Right side)**:** K6, P5, (K5, P5) across to last 6 sts, K6.

Loop a short piece of yarn around any stitch to mark Row 3 as **right** side.

Row 4: K1, P4, (K5, P5) across to last 2 sts, K2.

Rows 5 and 6: K1, P2, (K5, P5) across to last 4 sts, K4.

Row 7: K1, P4, (K5, P5) across to last 2 sts, K2.

Row 8: K6, P5, (K5, P5) across to last 6 sts, K6.

Rows 9 and 10: K1, P5, (K5, P5) across to last st, K1.

Row 11: K5, (P5, K5) across to last 2 sts, P1, K1.

Rows 12 and 13: K3, (P5, K5) across to last 4 sts, P3, K1.

Row 14: K5, (P5, K5) across to last 2 sts, P1, K1.

Row 15: K1, P5, (K5, P5) across to last st, K1.

Row 16: K6, P5, (K5, P5) across to last 6 sts, K6.

Repeat Rows 3-16 for pattern until piece measures 24{28-32}" / 61{71-81} cm, ending by working a **wrong** side row.

Cut Green.

FLAP

Rows 1-3: With Brown, knit across.

Row 4: K1, purl across.

Row 5 (Decrease row)**:** Slip 1 as if to **knit**, K1, PSSO, knit across: 86{76-86} sts.

Rows 6 thru 38{44-44}: Repeat Rows 4 and 5, 16{19-19} times; then repeat Row 4 once **more:** 70{57-67} sts.

Row 39{45-45}: (Slip 1 as if to **knit**, K1, PSSO) twice, knit across: 68{55-65} sts.

Row 40{46-46}: K1, purl across.

Repeat the last 2 rows, 30{24-29} times: 8{7-7} sts.

Bind off all sts in **purl**.

FINISHING

Steam Flap to block.

With **wrong** sides together, fold Body so that cast on edge meets base of Flap. With yarn needle and Green, whipstitch sides of Body together ***(Fig. 7, page 46)***. Insert pillow form, then stitch the cast on edge to the base of the Flap.

To anchor Flap, sew buttons to Flap **and** Body, beginning at bottom point and spacing buttons approximately ½" (12 mm) above point; sew remaining button to Body approximately 1¼" (3.75 cm) apart.

Tiny Mock Cables

INTERMEDIATE

Finished Sizes:
12" x 16" (30.5 cm x 40.5 cm)
14" x 14" (35.5 cm x 35.5 cm)
16" x 16" (40.5 cm x 40.5 cm)

Size Note: Instructions are written for 12" x 16" size, with sizes 14" x 14", and 16" x 16" in braces { }. Instructions will be easier to read if you circle all the numbers pertaining to your size. If only one number is given, it applies to all sizes.

SHOPPING LIST

Yarn (Medium Weight)

MEDIUM 4

[3.5 ounces, 210 yards (100 grams, 192 meters) per skein]:

- ☐ Tweed - 2{2-3} skeins
- ☐ Blue - 1 skein

Knitting Needles

- ☐ Straight, size 8 (5 mm) **or** size needed for gauge

Additional Supplies

- ☐ Pillow form - 12" x 16" {14" square - 16" square} / 30.5 cm x 40.5 cm {35.5 cm square - 40.5 cm square}
- ☐ Yarn needle
- ☐ $1^{1}/_{8}$" (30 mm) Buttons - 2

Techniques used:

- Slip 1, K1, PSSO ***(Fig. 1, page 44)***
- K2 tog ***(Fig. 2, page 44)***

GAUGE: In pattern,
23 sts and 25 rows = 4" (10 cm)

Gauge Swatch: 4" square (10 cm)
Cast on 23 sts.
Row 1: P3, (K2, P3) across.
Row 2: K3, (P2, K3) across.
Row 3: P3, ★ LT ***(Figs. C & D, page 32)***, P3; repeat from ★ across.
Row 4: K3, (P2, K3) across.
Rows 5 and 6: Repeat Rows 1 and 2.
Row 7: P3, ★ RT ***(Figs. E & F, page 32)***, P3; repeat from ★ across.
Row 8: K3, (P2, K3) across.
Rows 9-25: Repeat Rows 1-8 twice, then repeat Row 1 once **more**.
Bind off all sts in **purl**.

STITCH GUIDE

LEFT TWIST

(abbreviated LT) (uses 2 sts) Working behind first st on left needle, knit into the **back** of second st *(Fig. C)* making sure **not** to drop off, then knit the first st *(Fig. D)* letting both sts drop off needle.

Fig. C

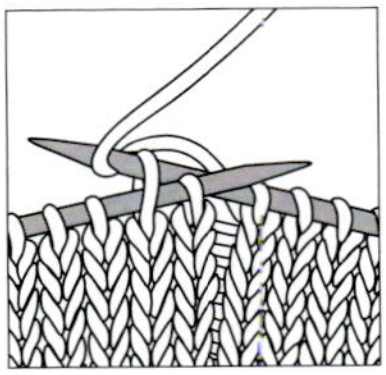

Fig. D

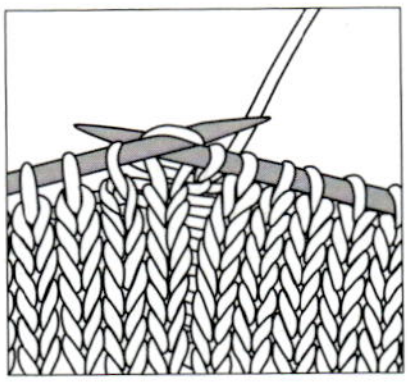

RIGHT TWIST

(abbreviated RT) (uses 2 sts) Knit second stitch on left needle *(Fig. E)* making sure **not** to drop off, then knit the first stitch *(Fig. F)* letting both sts drop off needle together.

Fig. E

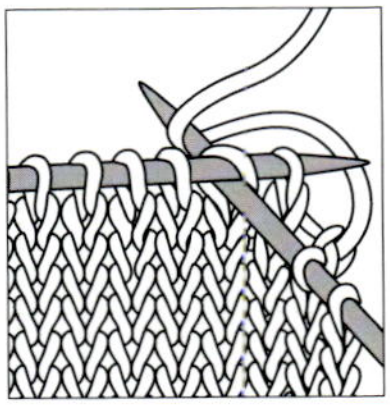

Fig. F

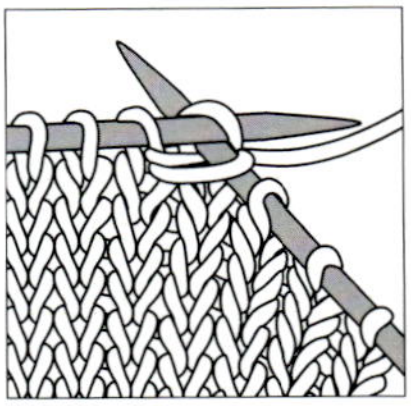

Pillow is made in one piece with the Body worked in pattern stitch and the Flap in Stockinette Stitch. Begin pillow at top edge, behind Flap.

BODY

With Tweed, cast on 95{80-95} sts.

Row 1 (Right side)**:** K1, P3, (K2, P3) across to last st, K1.

Loop a short piece of yarn around any stitch to mark Row 1 as **right** side.

Row 2: K4, P2, (K3, P2) across to last 4 sts, K4.

Row 3: K1, P3, (LT, P3) across to last st, K1.

Row 4: K4, P2, (K3, P2) across to last 4 sts, K4.

Rows 5 and 6: Repeat Rows 1 and 2.

Row 7: K1, P3, (RT, P3) across to last st, K1.

Row 8: K4, P2, (K3, P2) across to last 4 sts, K4.

Repeat Rows 1-8 for pattern until piece measures 24{28-32}" / 61{71-81} cm, ending by working a **wrong** side row.

Cut Tweed.

FLAP

Rows 1 and 2: With Blue, knit across.

Row 3 (Decrease row)**:** K1, slip 1 as if to **knit**, K1, PSSO, knit across to last 3 sts, K2 tog, K1: 93{78-93} sts.

Row 4: K1, purl across to last st, K1.

Row 5: Knit across.

Row 6: K1, purl across to last st, K1.

Rows 7-22: Repeat Rows 3-6, 4 times: 85{70-85} sts.

Rows 23-32: Repeat Rows 3 and 4, 5 times: 75{60-75} sts.

Row 33: K1, (slip 1 as if to **knit**, K1, PSSO) twice, knit across to last 5 sts, K2 tog twice, K1: 71{56-71} sts.

Row 34: K1, purl across to last st, K1.

Rows 35-46: Repeat Rows 33 and 34, 6 times: 47{32-47} sts.

Bind off all sts in **purl**.

EDGING

With **right** side facing and Blue, pick up 130{96-130} sts evenly spaced along end of rows and bound off edge of Flap.

Bind off all sts in **knit**.

FINISHING

Steam Flap to block.

With **wrong** sides together, fold Body so that cast on edge meets base of Flap. With yarn needle, whipstitch sides of Body together *(Fig. 7, page 46)*. Insert pillow form, then stitch the cast on edge to the base of the Flap.

To anchor Flap, sew buttons to Flap **and** Body above bound off edge and 1¼" (3 cm) on each side of the center.

Diagonal Texture Stripes

INTERMEDIATE

Finished Sizes:

12" x 16" (30.5 cm x 40.5 cm)
14" x 14" (35.5 cm x 35.5 cm)
16" x 16" (40.5 cm x 40.5 cm)

Size Note: Instructions are written for 12" x 16" size, with sizes 14" x 14", and 16" x 16" in braces { }. Instructions will be easier to read if you circle all the numbers pertaining to your size. If only one number is given, it applies to all sizes.

SHOPPING LIST

Yarn (Medium Weight) MEDIUM 4

[3.5 ounces, 177 yards (100 grams, 161 meters) per skein]:

- ☐ Pink - 3 skeins
- ☐ Purple - 1 skein

Knitting Needles

- ☐ Straight, size 8 (5 mm) **or** size needed for gauge

Additional Supplies

- ☐ Pillow form - 12" x 16" {14" square - 16" square} / 30.5 cm x 40.5 cm {35.5 cm square - 40.5 cm square}
- ☐ Yarn needle
- ☐ 1 1/8" (30 mm) Buttons - 2

GAUGE: In pattern,
22 sts and 26 rows = 4" (10 cm)

Gauge Swatch: 4" square (10 cm)
Cast on 22 sts.
Row 1: P6, K6, P6, K4.
Row 2: P3, K6, P6, K6. P1.
Row 3: K2, P6, K6, P6, K2.
Row 4: P1, K6, P6, K6, P3.
Row 5: K4, P6, K6, P6.
Row 6: K5, P6, K6, P5.
Row 7: K6, P6, K6, P4.
Row 8: K3, P6, K6, P6, K1.
Row 9: P2, K6, P6, K6, P2.
Row 10: K1, P6, K6, P6, K3.
Row 11: P4, K6, P6, K6.
Row 12: P5, K6, P6, K5.
Rows 13-26: Repeat Rows 1-12 once, then repeat Rows 1 and 2 once **more**.
Bind off all sts in **knit**.

Pillow is made in one piece with the Body worked in pattern stitch and the Flap in Stockinette Stitch. Begin pillow at top edge, behind Flap.

BODY

With Pink, cast on 68{80-92} sts.

Row 1 (Right side)**:** K7, P6, (K6, P6) across to last 7 sts, K7.

Loop a short piece of yarn around any stitch to mark Row 1 as **right** side.

Row 2: K1, P5, (K6, P6) across to last 2 sts, K2.

Row 3: K1, P2, (K6, P6) across to last 5 sts, K5.

Row 4: K1, P3, (K6, P6) across to last 4 sts, K4.

Row 5: K1, P4, (K6, P6) across to last 3 sts, K3.

Row 6: K1, P1, K6, (P6, K6) across.

Row 7: K1, P6, (K6, P6) across to last st, K1.

Row 8: K6, (P6, K6) across to last 2 sts, P1, K1.

Row 9: K3, (P6, K6) across to last 5 sts, P4, K1.

Row 10: K4, (P6, K6) across to last 4 sts, P3, K1.

Row 11: K5, (P6, K6) across to last 3 sts, P2, K1.

Row 12: K2, (P6, K6) across to last 6 sts, P5, K1.

Repeat Rows 1-12 for pattern until piece measures 32{28-32}" / 81{71-81} cm, ending by working a **wrong** side row.

Do **not** cut Pink.

FLAP

Rows 1-3: Knit across.

Row 4: K1, purl across to last st, K1.

Row 5: Knit across.

Rows 6 thru 32{26-28}: Repeat Rows 4 and 5, 13{10-11} times; then repeat Row 4 once **more**.

Cut Pink.

Row 33{27-29}: With Purple, knit across.

Row 34{28-30}: K1, purl across to last st, K1.

Row 35{29-31} thru 40{34-36}: Repeat last 2 rows, 3 times.

Bind off all sts in **purl**.

FINISHING

Steam Flap to block.

With **wrong** sides together, fold Body so that cast on edge meets base of Flap. With yarn needle and Pink, whipstitch sides of Body together ***(Fig. 7, page 46)***. Insert pillow form, then stitch the cast on edge to the base of the Flap.

To anchor Flap, sew buttons to Flap **and** Body, evenly spaced across Purple stripe.

Fisherman Rib

INTERMEDIATE

Finished Sizes:

12" x 16" (30.5 cm x 40.5 cm)
14" x 14" (35.5 cm x 35.5 cm)
16" x 16" (40.5 cm x 40.5 cm)

Size Note: Instructions are written for 12" x 16" size, with sizes 14" x 14", and 16" x 16" in braces { }. Instructions will be easier to read if you circle all the numbers pertaining to your size. If only one number is given, it applies to all sizes.

SHOPPING LIST

Yarn (Medium Weight) MEDIUM 4

[3.5 ounces, 210 yards (100 grams, 192 meters) per skein]:

☐ Brown - 2{2-3} skeins
Orange - 1{1-2} skein(s)

Knitting Needles

☐ Straight, size 9 (5.5 mm) **or** size needed for gauge

Additional Supplies

☐ Pillow form - 12" x 16" {14" square - 16" square} / 30.5 cm x 40.5 cm {35.5 cm square - 40.5 cm square}
☐ Yarn needle
☐ 1¼" (30 mm) Button - 1
☐ $^{7}/_{8}$" (30 mm) Button - 1

Techniques used:

- Slip 1, K1, PSSO ***(Fig. 1, page 44)***
- K2 tog ***(Fig. 2, page 44)***

GAUGE: In pattern,
18 sts and 36 rows = 4" (10 cm)

Gauge Swatch:
4¼"w x 4"h (11 x 10 cm)
Cast on 19 sts.
Work same as Body for 36 rows.
Bind off all sts in pattern.

Pillow is made in one piece with the Body worked in pattern stitch and the Flap in Stockinette Stitch. Begin pillow at top edge, behind Flap.

STITCH GUIDE

KNIT IN STITCH BELOW

(uses one st)
Insert right needle into st **below** next stitch ***(Fig. G)***, YO and pull through stitch letting both sts drop off needle.

Fig. G

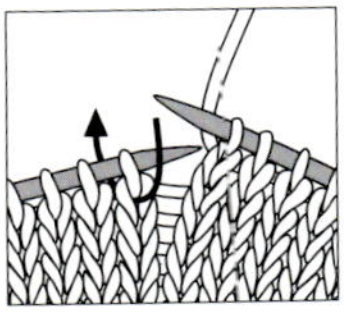

BODY

With Brown, cast on 73{63-73} sts.

Row 1: K2, P1, (K1, P1) across to last 2 sts, K2.

Row 2: K1, P1, (K1 in st below, P1) across to last st, K1.

Row 3: K1, K1 in st below, (P1, K1 in st below) across to last st, K1.

Repeat Rows 2 and 3 for pattern until piece measures 24{28-32}" / 61{71-81} cm, ending by working a **wrong** side row.

Cut Brown.

FLAP

Rows 1-3: With Orange, knit across.

Row 4: K1, purl across to last st, K1.

Both sides of Flap are worked at the same time, using separate yarn for **each** side.

Row 5 (Right side - Dividing row)**:** K 35{30-35}, K2 tog; with second yarn, knit across: 36{31-36} sts **each** side.

Row 6: K1, purl across to last st, K1; with second yarn, K1, purl across to last st, K1.

Row 7 (Decrease row)**:** Knit across to last 3 sts, K2 tog, K1; with second yarn, K1, slip 1 as if to **knit**, K1, PSSO, knit across: 35{30-35} sts **each** side.

Rows 8 thru 22{26-22}: Repeat Rows 6 and 7, 7{9-7} times; then repeat Row 6 once **more**: 28{21-28} sts **each** side.

Row 23{27-23}: Knit across; with second yarn, knit across.

Row 24{28-24}: K1, purl across to last st, K1; with second yarn, K1, purl across to last st, K1.

Rows 25{29-25} thru 30{36-40}: Repeat last 2 rows,3{4-8} times.

Bind off all sts in **purl**.

FINISHING

Steam Flap to block.

With **wrong** sides together, fold Body so that cast on edge meets base of Flap. With yarn needle and Brown, whipstitch sides of Body together *(Fig. 7, page 46)*. Insert pillow form, then stitch the cast on edge to the base of the Flap.

To anchor Flap, sew smaller buttons to Flap **and** Body at inside corners of Flap; sew larger button at point of Flap.

General Instructions

ABBREVIATIONS

cm	centimeters
K	knit
mm	millimeters
P	purl
PSSO	pass slipped stitch over
st(s)	stitch(es)
tbl	through back loop(s)
tog	together
WYB	with yarn in back
WYF	with yarn in front
YO	yarn over

KNIT TERMINOLOGY		
UNITED STATES		INTERNATIONAL
gauge	=	tension
bind off	=	cast off
yarn over (YO)	=	yarn forward (yfwd) or yarn around needle (yrn)

SYMBOLS & TERMS

★ — work instructions following ★ as **many** more times as indicated in addition to the first time.

( ) or [ ] — work enclosed instructions **as many** times as specified by the number immediately following **or** work all enclosed instructions in the stitch or space indicated **or** contains explanatory remarks.

colon (:) — the numbers given after a colon at the end of a row denote the number of stitches you should have on that row.

Yarn Weight Symbol & Names	LACE 0	SUPER FINE 1	FINE 2	LIGHT 3	MEDIUM 4	BULKY 5	SUPER BULKY 6
Type of Yarns in Category	Fingering, size 10 crochet thread	Sock, Fingering, Baby	Sport, Baby	DK, Light Worsted	Worsted, Afghan, Aran	Chunky, Craft, Rug	Bulky, Roving
Knit Gauge Range* in Stockinette St to 4" (10 cm)	33-40** sts	27-32 sts	23-26 sts	21-24 sts	16-20 sts	12-15 sts	6-11 sts
Advised Needle Size Range	000-1	1 to 3	3 to 5	5 to 7	7 to 9	9 to 11	11 and larger

*GUIDELINES ONLY: The chart above reflects the most commonly used gauges and needle sizes for specific yarn categories.

** Lace weight yarns are usually knitted on larger needles to create lacy openwork patterns. Accordingly, a gauge range is difficult to determine. Always follow the gauge stated in your pattern.

KNITTING NEEDLES																
U.S.	0	1	2	3	4	5	6	7	8	9	10	10½	11	13	15	17
U.K.	13	12	11	10	9	8	7	6	5	4	3	2	1	00	000	---
Metric - mm	2	2.25	2.75	3.25	3.5	3.75	4	4.5	5	5.5	6	6.5	8	9	10	12.75

GAUGE

Exact gauge is essential for proper size. Before beginning your project, make a sample swatch approximately 4" (10 cm) square in the yarn and needles specified. After completing the swatch, measure it, counting your stitches and rows carefully. If your swatch is larger or smaller than specified, make another, changing needle size to get the correct gauge. Keep trying until you find the size needles that will give you the specified gauge. Once proper gauge is obtained, measure width of the piece approximately ever 3" (7.5 cm) to be sure gauge remains consistent.

HINTS

As in all knitted pieces, good finishing techniques make a big difference in the quality of the piece. Do not tie knots.

Always start a new ball at the beginning of a row, leaving ends long enough to weave in later.

Make a habit of taking care of loose ends as you work. Thread a yarn needle with the yarn end. With **wrong** side facing, weave the needle through several stitches, then reverse the direction and weave it back through several stitches. When the ends are secure, clip them off close to the work.

BLOCKING

Follow instructions on yarn label or block as follows:

Wool: Steam flap, supporting weight of iron at all times.

Allow to dry flat, away from heat or sunlight.

Synthetic and blends: Submerge flap in cool water. Roll piece in a clean terry towel and gently press out the excess moisture. Lay flat and allow to dry completely, away from heat and sunlight.

BEGINNER	Projects for first-time knitters using basic knit and purl stitches. Minimal shaping.
EASY	Projects using basic stitches, repetitive stitch patterns, simple color changes, and simple shaping and finishing.
INTERMEDIATE	Projects with a variety of stitches, such as basic cables and lace, simple intarsia, double-pointed needles and knitting in the round needle techniques, mid-level shaping and finishing.
EXPERIENCED	Projects using advanced techniques and stitches, such as short rows, fair isle, more intricate intarsia, cables, lace patterns, and numerous color changes.

DECREASES

SLIP 1, KNIT 1, PASS SLIPPED STITCH OVER

(abbreviated slip 1, K1, PSSO)

Slip one stitch as if to **knit**. Knit the next stitch. With the left needle, bring the slipped stitch over the knit stitch ***(Fig. 1)*** and off the needle.

Fig. 1

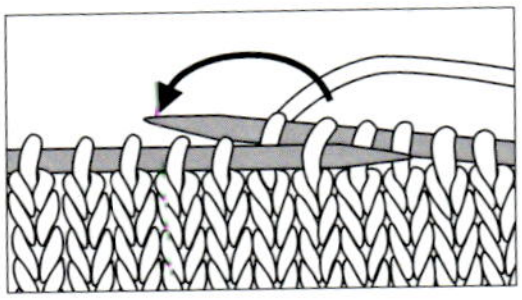

KNIT 2 TOGETHER

(abbreviated K2 tog)

Insert the right needle into the **front** of the first two stitches on the left needle as if to **knit** ***(Fig. 2)***, then knit them together as if they were one stitch.

Fig. 2

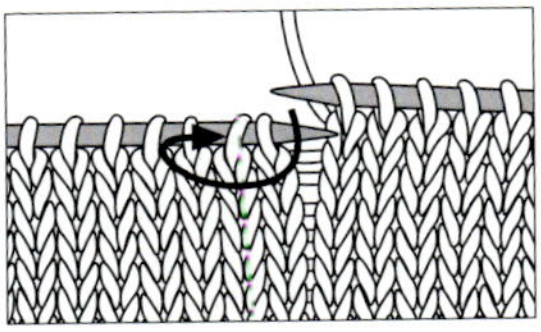

KNIT 2 TOGETHER THROUGH BACK LOOP

(abbreviated K2 tog tbl)

Insert the right needle into the **back** of first two stitches on the left needle from **front** to **back** ***(Fig. 3)***, then knit them together as if they were one stitch.

Fig. 3

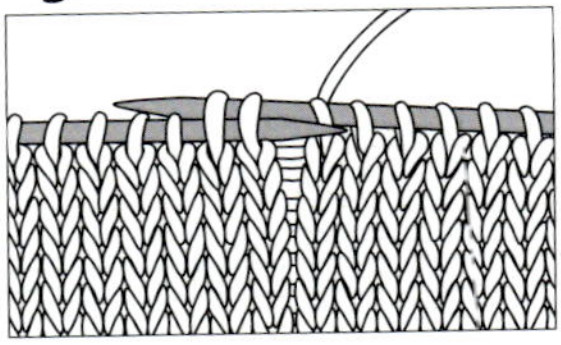

PURL 2 TOGETHER

(abbreviated P2 tog)

Insert the right needle into the **front** of the first two stitches on the left needle as if to **purl** ***(Fig. 4)***, then purl them together as if they were one stitch.

Fig. 4

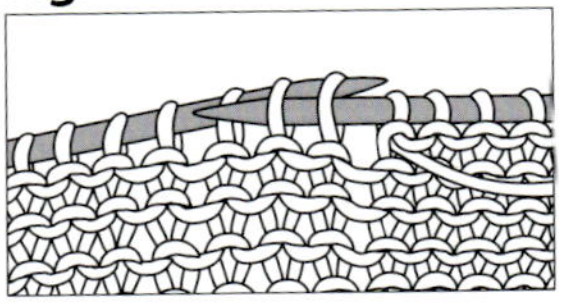

PURL 3 TOGETHER

(abbreviated P3 tog)

Insert the right needle into the **front** of the first three stitches on the left needle as if to **purl** ***(Fig. 5)***, then purl them together.

Fig. 5

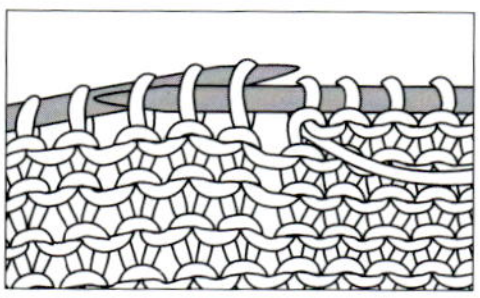

YARN OVERS

(abbreviated YO)

After a purl stitch, before a purl stitch

Take yarn **over** the right hand needle to the back, then forward **under** it, so that it is now in position to purl the next stitch ***(Fig. 6a)***.

Fig. 6a

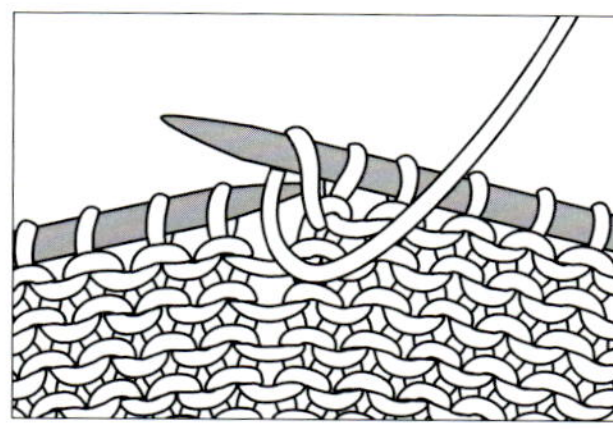

After a knit stitch, before a purl stitch

Bring yarn forward **between** the needles, then back **over** the top of the right hand needle and forward **between** the needles again, so that it is now in position to purl the next stitch ***(Fig. 6b)***.

Fig. 6b

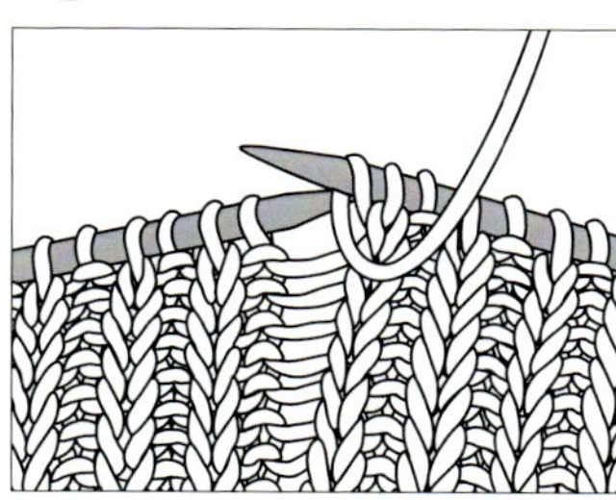

WHIPSTITCH

With **wrong** sides together, sew through both pieces once to secure the beginning of the seam, leaving an ample yarn end to weave in later. Insert the needle from right to left through one strand on each piece ***(Fig. 7)***. Bring the needle around and insert it from right to left through the next strand on both pieces.

Repeat along the edge, being careful to match stitches and rows.

Fig. 7

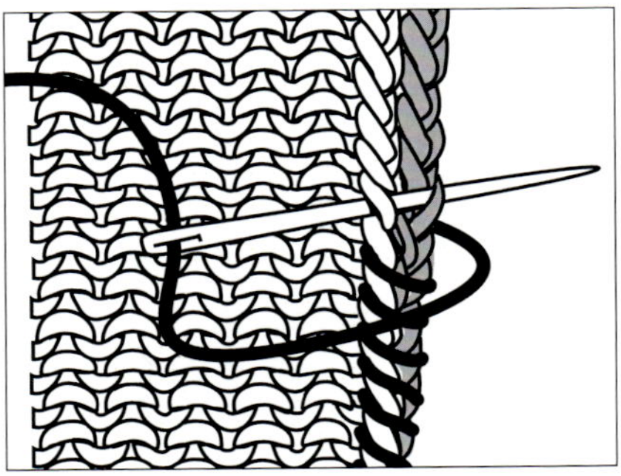

Yarn Information

The items in this leaflet were made using medium weight yarn. Any brand of medium weight yarn may be used. It is best to refer to the yardage/meters when determining how many balls or skeins to purchase. Remember, to achieve the same look, it is the weight of yarn that is important, not the brand of yarn. For your convenience, listed below are the specific yarns used to create our photography models.

TWO COLOR SLIP STITCH
Patons® Classic Wool Worsted
#77223 Lemongrass
#00225 Dark Grey Mix

TWISTED GARTER STITCH
Lion Brand® Fisherman's Wool
#123 Oatmeal
#201 Maple Tweed

BASKETWEAVE
Patons® Classic Wool Worsted
#224 Grey Mix
#77044 Mercury

BROKEN RIB STITCH
Patons® Classic Wool Worsted
#77308 Wisteria
#00212 Royal Purple

STAR STITCH
Lion Brand® Wool-Ease®
#099 Fisherman
#153 Black

LACE RIBBING
Patons® Classic Wool Worsted
#77201 Aquarium

ZIG ZAG ANGLES
Lion Brand® Wool-Ease®
#174 Avocado
#129 Cocoa

TINY MOCK CABLES
Patons® Classic Wool Tweeds
#84008 Aran Tweed
Patons® Classic Wool
#77115 New Denim

DIAGONAL TEXTURE STRIPES
Patons® Classic Wool Worsted
#77402 Magenta
#212 Royal Purple

FISHERMAN RIB
Patons® Classic Wool Tweeds
#84013 Chestnut Tweed
Patons® Classic Wool
#77605 Pumpkin

Production Team: Technical Writer/Editor – Lois J Long;
Editorial Writer - Susan Fritz Wiles; Senior Graphic Artist - Mark Hawkins;
Photo Stylist - Christy Myers; and Photographer - Mark Mathews.

Made in U.S.A.